The Lady of
Ten Thousand Names

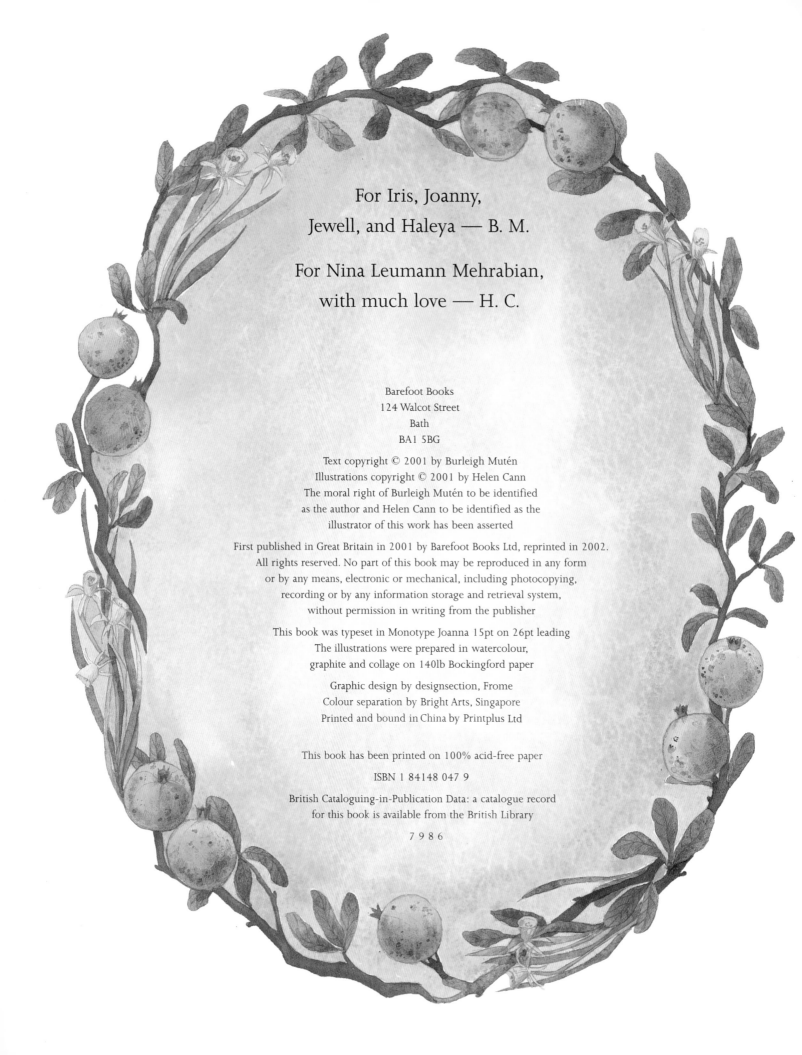

For Iris, Joanny,
Jewell, and Haleya — B. M.

For Nina Leumann Mehrabian,
with much love — H. C.

Barefoot Books
124 Walcot Street
Bath
BA1 5BG

This book was typeset in Monotype Joanna 15pt on 26pt leading
The illustrations were prepared in watercolour,
graphite and collage on 140lb Bockingford paper

Graphic design by designsection, Frome
Colour separation by Bright Arts, Singapore
Printed and bound in China by Printplus Ltd

This book has been printed on 100% acid-free paper

ISBN 1 84148 047 9

British Cataloguing-in-Publication Data: a catalogue record
for this book is available from the British Library

7 9 8 6

The Lady of Ten Thousand Names

Goddess Stories from Many Cultures

Retold by **BURLEIGH MUTÉN**

Illustrated by **HELEN CANN**

Barefoot Books
Celebrating Art and Story

CONTENTS

FOREWORD

Goddesses have been part of mythology all over the Earth from the beginning of time. Goddess worship dates back to the Stone Age, some 35,000 years ago. From Japan to North America and from Africa to Wales, the oldest stories inform us of powerful women who gave birth to humanity, healed their people, and blessed them with many gifts. During the past quarter century, more and more women and men have become aware of the ancient female deity. Now, as we enter a new millennium, it is time for these stories to be shared again with our daughters and sons.

The stories I have selected for this volume are based on traditional tales and sacred texts. As old as they are, their themes still offer relevant issues for children and adults today. From Egypt, *The Lady of Ten Thousand Names* is the story of sibling rivalry and loyalty. From China, *The Princess Who Became a Goddess* is the story of an exceptional child who has the courage to defy her parents' wishes so that she can follow the path of her heart and, later in life, to forgive them when they are in need. *We Are All One Family* is a tale from the Lakota Sioux of North America, reminding us to show respect for all members of Mother Earth's family. From the ancient tradition of Wales, *Mother of Magic* shows us the miraculous power of a mother's love for her child.

A darker aspect of the goddess is revealed in the Scandinavian story of *The Blessing Necklace*, for here we meet a woman who is willing to create war on Earth in order to get what she wants. By contrast, in the Japanese tale, *Ama-terasu's Mirror*, this goddess takes drastic measures to escape from her brother's jealousy and violence. In the Yoruba tale, *The Great Mother*, we see how quickly life becomes unbalanced when the feminine principle is excluded from the creative process. Finally, in the story from the Greek legend of *Persephone, Demeter and Hekate*, we see the loyalty and love of three generations of women who refuse to be dominated by men.

At a time in history when young girls are encouraged to strive for their dreams, it is an honour to offer these ancient stories about goddesses who are models of female leadership, authority and wisdom. As we become more aware of our spiritual heritage through these sacred stories and images which revere women, we are all, young and old alike, more able to embody and share our personal power.

Burleigh Mutén
Amherst, Massachusetts, 2001

Isis

EGYPTIAN

Isis, whose name means 'Ultimate Queen', was worshipped in Egypt for over seven thousand years. She was called 'The Lady of Ten Thousand Names' because all other goddesses were believed to be aspects of Isis. She knew how to use plants as medicine, and she was especially famous as a healer of children. She also taught women how to weave, spin and cultivate their gardens.

This is the story of Isis's love and loyalty to her husband, Osiris, and of the birth of her son, Horus.

THE LADY OF
TEN THOUSAND NAMES

In the beginning there was Nut, the Night Sky. Nut gave the Earth to her first child, Isis. 'These lands are yours,' Nut proclaimed, 'to protect and to nourish.' Nut gave the Waters of Earth to her second child, Osiris.

From the day he was born, Isis loved her little brother. She carried him to the River Nile and to each water hole in the desert so he would know all the waters in Egypt. Every night, Isis held Osiris on her lap as the sun glowed pink and purple across the sky. Together, they watched the stars on Nut's dress glow and sparkle above them.

Later Nut gave birth to twins, a girl named Nebthet and a boy named Set. From the day Set was born, it was clear that he was a different sort

of child. His hair was bright red, unlike the gleaming black hair of his siblings, and his skin was pale pink, unlike the soft brown skin of everyone else. Set was a small child, and he was rambunctious and loud. 'You will rule over the Dead,' Nut said to the twins. Nebthet was pleased with this, but Set always yearned for whatever Osiris, his older brother, had.

When they were grown, Isis ruled over Egypt as queen, and Osiris was king. Isis loved working in her garden. She collected dried leaves, roots and blossoms, and from these she made soothing ointments and healing teas. One day, the sun's rays scorched every plant in Isis's garden. Osiris saw how this saddened Isis and he shook his fists at the sun, shouting, 'I will kill the sun! No one shall steal my queen's joy.'

'You can't kill the sun,' Isis laughed. 'All beings on Earth must have sunlight and water to live. You know that. My garden needs its own river, that's all.'

'Then your garden shall have its own river,' pronounced Osiris. 'Your garden shall have the River Nile!' He called for a group of servants to dig a long, deep ditch from the Nile through the desert to Isis's garden. Crowds of people gathered to see what would happen, and, indeed, the River Nile poured into the ditch and flowed directly to the queen's withered garden. The leaves of her plants turned green again and flowered.

Isis smiled and hugged Osiris and the people cheered. Set covered his ears. He wanted the people to cheer for him. More than ever, Set wanted to be king.

He invited Osiris to a grand celebration. 'Everyone loves you, Osiris,' Set said to his brother. 'Let me show you how much I love you.'

That night, Isis dreamed about Set's soldiers surrounding Osiris. 'Be watchful, my beloved,' she warned him. 'Set has envied you all his life. Be aware of his intentions.'

'You are wise to remind me,' said Osiris. 'I will watch Set.'

At Set's palace, the tables were covered with dishes of fresh fruit and meat. As always, the guests were happy to see their king. When the last moon cakes had been eaten and the guests were woozy with beer, Set pulled the cloth from the table where he and Osiris were sitting. Beneath

it was a jewelled coffin, dazzling with lapis and gold. 'He who fits this coffin shall have it for his own,' announced Set.

One by one, Set's guests climbed into the fancy coffin. It was too narrow. It was too wide. It was too long or too short for any of them. Last of all, it was the king's turn. Everyone cheered as Osiris walked

towards the coffin. Osiris hesitated. He remembered Isis's words. 'Could this be a trick?' he wondered. He looked at Set. The guests were still cheering. His younger brother had clearly made this beautiful gift for him. He couldn't disappoint Set or the cheering guests. Osiris climbed into the coffin and leaned back. It was a perfect fit. Osiris smiled at Set. 'Why, this bejewelled coffin is apparently for me, Little Brother.'

'Of course it is, you trusting fool,' said Set, slamming its lid shut.

'Let me out!' Osiris bellowed. 'In the name of the queen, let me out of this box!'

But no one listened. Set's soldiers surrounded the coffin and carried it to the river's edge.

Set was pleased. 'Let him go,' he yelled. 'Let the King of Yesterday be gone forever!'

Isis heard a ringing in her ears. Something was wrong. In the shadows and sunlight, she saw a vision of Set's soldiers surrounding Osiris. She flung her arms above her head and said her true name, Au Set. Glistening feathered wings instantly appeared where her arms had been. Then, as she swooped her wings down to her sides, Isis became a miniature winged woman the size of a swallow, and then she became a swallow. Hopping into the air, she soared towards Set's palace.

Inside the coffin, Osiris felt the river's swift current carry him rapidly downstream. 'I should have refused Set's beer,' he said to himself.

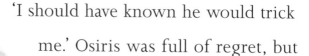

'I should have known he would trick me.' Osiris was full of regret, but he was not afraid. He knew Isis would find him.

Many days passed. Isis flew through the thick hot air. She flew against the wind. Osiris, still confined in his coffin, began to weaken from hunger and thirst. The riverbed took an abrupt turn, and the current quickened. The coffin crashed into the trunk of a tamarisk tree. Osiris was jolted from one side of the coffin to the other, hitting his head and falling into the sleep of death. The tree folded its bark around the coffin, and as time passed, the coffin was completely concealed within the tree.

When Isis got there, the tamarisk tree was nothing but a wide, flat stump. A woodcarver had cut it down and taken the wood. Isis rested in the reeds near the tamarisk stump that night, and as she dreamed, she saw Osiris lying inside the coffin within a tall, wooden pillar at a palace nearby. She awoke with a start.

In the morning, when the lady of the palace saw a swallow frantically circling one of her pillars, she placed a bowl of water on the ground.

'What is your trouble, little one?' she asked.

Isis flew to the rim of the bowl. She hopped into the water and bathed her feathers. As she opened her wings, she returned to the shape of a miniature winged woman. Then, in a blink, she resumed her full size. The woman fell to her knees. 'Lady of the Land! What brings you here?' she gasped.

Isis explained Set's betrayal of Osiris. 'I am sure my king lies prisoner within this pillar,' said Isis. The woman immediately called for her servants to cut down the pillar and split it open. There, indeed, was the lapis and gold coffin, and there, indeed, was the corpse of Osiris. Isis wailed with grief. She put the coffin on to a barge and began the long journey back up the river to bury Osiris.

Isis kept Osiris's body hidden in the swamps of the river delta. She bathed him with cool water. 'I will be right back,' she said to the corpse, as if Osiris could hear her. 'I must gather the herbs for embalming your body, then I will take you to the Land of the Dead.'

Now Set happened to be hunting by moonlight that night. When he saw the gleaming gold coffin floating in the reeds, he couldn't believe his eyes. 'This cannot be!' he growled. 'I am having a nightmare!' he said, striding towards the coffin. 'How could Isis have found him and brought him here?' Set cried, reaching for his sword. 'She won't find you now,' he snarled as he cut Osiris's body into fourteen pieces. 'She won't find you now!' he sneered as he threw

each piece into the river. 'Now I am finished with you forever!'

Isis felt her heart twitch. Something was wrong. She ran back to the river. As soon as she saw the empty coffin, she cried with fury. She knew exactly what had happened. Lifting her hands above her head, she said her true name and dived into the river. Her outstretched legs became the sleek, strong tail of a giant perch and she sped through the waters of the Nile, searching for Osiris.

Piece by piece, Isis gathered up each part of Osiris's body. Piece by piece, she and her sister, Nebthet, put him back together. Isis sang the 'Chant for New Life'. She sang all day, and she sang all night. Finally, Osiris opened his eyes. He could barely lift his head. His voice was a whisper. Isis wrapped her arms gently around him and loved him. Then Osiris died. There was nothing Isis could do to revive him now.

She sang as she embalmed his body with ointments. She sang as she placed him on Nebthet's barge. She sang all the way to the Underworld.

As Isis left Osiris, she felt their child growing inside her. 'The new king!' she thought to herself, and she smiled. Knowing that Set would be jealous of her son, Isis stayed in the desert until Horus was born. Horus was a weak baby.

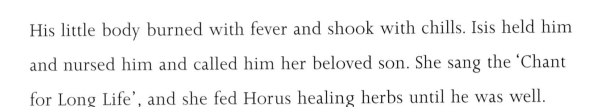

His little body burned with fever and shook with chills. Isis held him and nursed him and called him her beloved son. She sang the 'Chant for Long Life', and she fed Horus healing herbs until he was well.

Every evening, as the sky turned pink and purple, Isis held Horus on her lap and they watched the stars sparkle on Nut's dress. As soon as Horus could walk, Isis took him on long journeys to explore the Earth and its waters. She taught her son the names of every plant in Egypt. She showed him how and when to harvest their seeds, roots and blossoms. She taught him how to heal with plant medicine. She taught him every magical chant she knew.

Of course, Set was jealous of Horus. When Horus was grown, Set challenged him to fight for the throne. 'Set is old,' said Isis. 'You are a strong young man, my son. You are the King of Egypt. You have nothing to fear.'

Isis was right. Horus and Set fought for the throne, and Horus overpowered his uncle.

Isis ruled as queen with her son Horus for thousands of years. Her power to heal and her unending love made her one of the most beloved goddesses of all time.

Kuan Yin
CHINESE

Kuan Yin, whose name means 'She Who Hears the Cries of the World', has been worshipped for centuries as the goddess of kindness, mercy and grace. She is also known as 'The Lady Who Brings Children'. It is said that if you are in danger and you call out her name, she will come to your rescue. If you are sick and you pray to Kuan Yin, she will heal you. Kuan Yin gives children to people who have none, and she brings peace to the battlefield. This is the story of how Kuan Yin, who was a king's daughter, became a goddess.

THE PRINCESS WHO
BECAME A GODDESS

Once, long ago, there were a queen and king who had two
daughters. They loved their little girls, but a king in China without
a son was considered a cursed man. A king with no son was the last of
his line. The queen and king prayed to the gods for a son. At last, as the
queen gave birth to her third child, the Earth trembled and the lovely
scent of lotus blossoms filled the air for miles around. The clouds glowed
with the colours of the rainbow and everyone realised that a holy person
had been born. Everyone rejoiced but the queen and king, for their
third child was a girl.

Maio Shan was as graceful and polite as her older sisters, but there
was no doubt in anyone's mind that she was different. Maio Shan

refused to wear fancy silk robes. 'I will wear flax, like the simple folk wear,' she insisted. Nor would she eat rich food. 'A bowl of rice, please,' she would say with a smile, bowing her head.

Maio Shan had two passions: praying for the poor and sick, and nursing stray, underfed animals back to health. The queen and king shook their heads. They did not understand their third daughter. They tolerated her peculiar ways until Maio Shan was grown and she refused to marry.

'I need sons-in-law to rule my kingdom,' the king said sternly. 'You will marry the man of my choice!'

'Please, Father, let my sisters have husbands. Allow me to live a life of quiet prayer,' Maio Shan begged.

The queen put her arm around her daughter's shoulders. 'You are a princess, Maio Shan. You are no longer a child. Your father is king. You must respect his wishes.'

Maio Shan sighed. 'If I must marry,' she conceded, 'I will marry a doctor who will heal the sick and help the poor.'

The king pounded the table with his fist. 'A doctor!' he shouted. 'How can a doctor defend a palace? What does a doctor know about ruling a kingdom?'

'Father, my sisters will give you sons-in-law. I beg you, allow me to live in a nunnery,' pleaded Maio Shan. 'I will be your happiest daughter if I can spend my days praying for the good of all people.'

The queen saw that Maio Shan would not change her mind. She urged the king to consider the nunnery in the mountains. The king's face turned red with rage, but he called for the Abbess. 'Give my daughter the most difficult and demeaning tasks,' he insisted. 'She will come to her senses when she sees what a nun's life is really like.'

The Abbess saw kindness in Maio Shan's eyes. She could tell that the princess was sincere, but she had to obey the king's orders. She gave Maio Shan the tasks of scrubbing the floors and carrying firewood. Maio Shan was not discouraged. She had prayed for a simple life. She did not complain when her hands blistered and bled as she carried water from the stream. She did not complain when her back ached as she carried wood to the kitchen stove.

When the king received news of how happy Maio Shan was at the nunnery, he was furious. He paced back and forth in his throne room, thinking hard, and then he called for the commander of his army.

'Burn the nunnery down!' he ordered. 'Burn it down to the ground!'

The king's soldiers surrounded the nunnery, ignited their arrows and let them fly. In a matter of minutes, the building was ablaze. When Maio Shan realised that her own father's army had started the blaze, she was horrified. She ran directly to the statue of Buddha, fell on to her knees and prayed. 'Great Spirit of the Universe, hear my prayer. I am the daughter of a king just as you were the son of a king. I have left the royal life to pray for the world just as you left the royal life to pray for the world. Help me rescue my sisters in this house of prayer.'

Dark clouds instantly gathered over the nunnery, rumbling and pouring rivers of rain from the sky. Within minutes, the fire was out and the nuns were unharmed. Realising that divine forces opposed his army, the commander ordered a retreat.

This news enraged the king. He threw his dagger into the wall. 'Capture the woman who has been an enormous problem for me from the day of her birth,' he commanded. 'Capture my daughter and execute her in the morning.' The king's soldiers had no choice. They went back to the nunnery, bound Maio Shan, and carried her to the king's dungeon.

Once again the queen begged Maio Shan to marry the man of her father's choice, and once again Maio Shan refused.

Now, Hsi Wang Mu, the Queen Mother of the West, looked down to Earth and overheard the king's orders. She sighed with sadness and called for the Spirit of the Execution Square to rescue Maio Shan. 'Use all means

of magic to spare Maio Shan,'
she ordered.

In the morning, as the first
light of dawn began to
brighten the sky, the
princess was led into
the Execution Square.
The king's soldiers
stood to attention
around her. Maio
Shan was not afraid.
She was ready to die.
The executioner
lifted his glistening
sword above her head.
A soft white light
surrounded Maio Shan.
The sword blade slid from
its hilt and fell to the
ground. The executioner

grabbed his spear but it melted like butter in the heat of his hand.
Desperate to fulfil his king's order, the executioner pulled the sash
from his own waist and strangled Maio Shan.

As the princess breathed her last breath, a huge tiger leaped over the king's soldiers, pushing the executioner to the ground with a thud. The tiger quickly slid beneath Maio Shan's body and bounded away from the square with the princess on its back. As soon as they were in the shaded forest, the tiger laid Maio Shan down on a bed of ferns and gently placed a peach of immortality into her mouth.

When Maio Shan woke from the deep sleep of the dead, she found herself in the land of the gods. She spent so much time looking down to Earth, assisting those who were in trouble, she was given a new name, Kuan Yin, which means 'She Who Hears the Cries of the World'.

One day, Kuan Yin heard the cries of her own father, the king, who was in great pain. The old man's withered body was aflame with red streaks that burned day and night. No doctor had a cure or even a salve that would soothe the king's disease.

Later that day, a monk appeared at the palace, claiming to have a cure for the mysterious disease that tormented the king. As the humble monk approached him, the king laughed out loud. 'What can a monk do for me?' he demanded. 'How dare you approach the king with false claims!'

The monk bowed slowly, lowering his eyes. 'You will be well,' he said, 'if you do as I say, Sire. First, you will need an eye and an arm from a person whose heart is full of pure love. The eye and the arm must be given freely for the sake of your healing. Put the eye and the arm into this salve and it will cure your disease.'

'Preposterous!' yelled the king. 'Execute this fraud. There is no person on Earth whose heart is full of pure love.'

'You are mistaken, Sire,' said the monk, as the king's soldiers pushed him out of the room. 'There is a woman,' he called over his shoulder, 'who holds no anger in her heart. She will answer your prayer if you call her by name.'

'Stop!' called the king. 'What is her name?'

'Kuan Yin,' replied the monk.

'Kuan Yin!' called the king. 'Help me, Kuan Yin! I am wild from this burning! Help me!'

'My father has been harsh,' thought Kuan Yin to herself. 'He has been cruel and unfair.' But her heart was full of pure love. She could not refuse his request. In a matter of seconds, she appeared at the side of his bed in a ray of sunlight that streamed into his room.

'It can't be!' gasped the queen, recognising her daughter at once.

'Quick! Give me one of your eyes and one of your arms,' demanded the king, not even looking up at the goddess's face.

'Of course,' she replied.

Then to everyone's amazement, Kuan Yin

plucked out one of her eyes and pulled off one of her arms, collapsing on the floor.

The king slathered the salve all over his body and sighed with relief. For the first time in months, he was not in pain. For the first time in months, he began to feel at peace. Then he noticed the queen bending over the goddess.

'My daughter! Can it be Maio Shan?' he exclaimed joining his wife at her side.

Kuan Yin smiled and placed her palm on her father's shoulder. 'Yes, Father. I have come to heal you.'

The Earth trembled, and great rainbow-coloured clouds gathered over the palace. The lovely scent of lotus blossoms filled the air, and flowers rained down on to the Earth. As soon as the air cleared, the king and the queen saw their daughter floating over her father's bed. Her spirit body had one thousand eyes and one thousand arms. Kuan Yin leaned over her mother and kissed her. She kissed the old king. Then she rose slowly into the sky like the round golden moon, spreading her glowing light all over the Earth.

The queen and king cried in each other's arms. They were astounded to know that their daughter had become the great goddess of kindness and healing, Kuan Yin. From that day on, they shared their wealth with all the people in their kingdom. No one ever went hungry, and healers were available for all the sick.

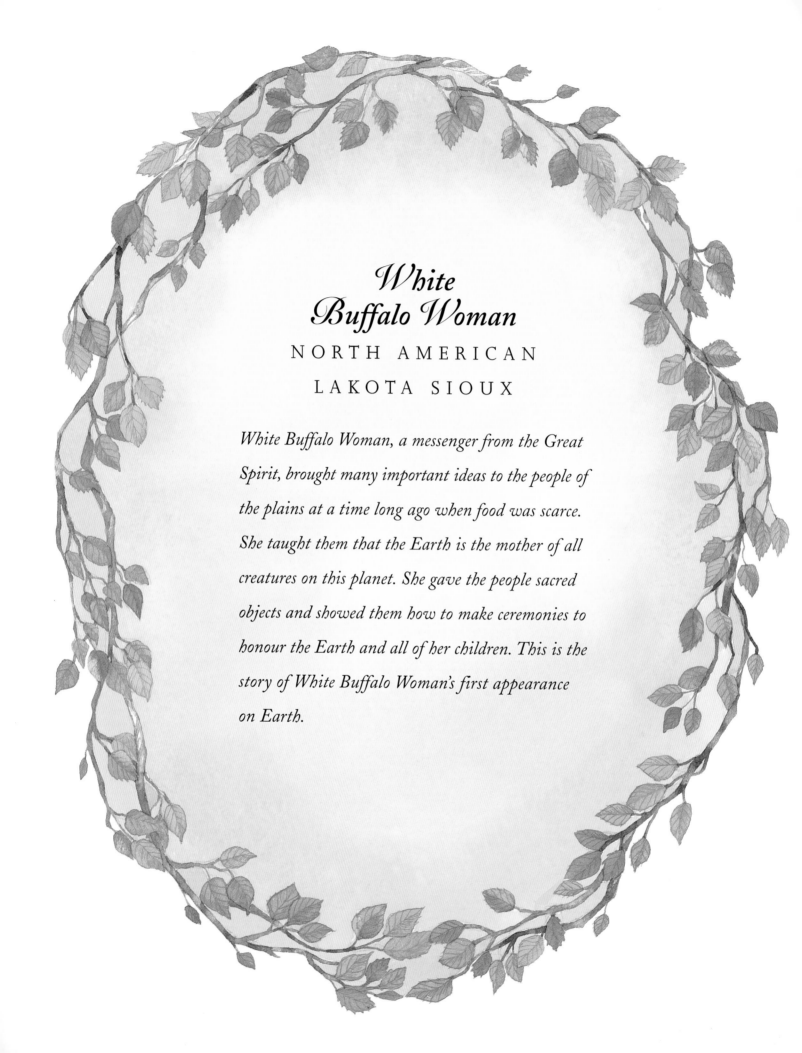

White Buffalo Woman

NORTH AMERICAN

LAKOTA SIOUX

White Buffalo Woman, a messenger from the Great Spirit, brought many important ideas to the people of the plains at a time long ago when food was scarce. She taught them that the Earth is the mother of all creatures on this planet. She gave the people sacred objects and showed them how to make ceremonies to honour the Earth and all of her children. This is the story of White Buffalo Woman's first appearance on Earth.

WE ARE ALL ONE FAMILY

Once, long ago in the time before we were born, there were two brothers who took their bows and arrows on to the plains looking for game. The older brother was a thoughtful young man. He was very observant and noticed the needs of others. The younger brother, however, always thought of himself first.

On this particular morning, as the sun painted the plains with rosy, pink light, the older brother paused to admire the beautiful sunrise. The younger brother was glad for a moment's rest. As they gazed out over the wide rolling plains, the older one noticed an unusual cloud of dust in the distance. It seemed to glow with a white light of its own, and it seemed to be whirling quickly in their direction. Not so much

as a breeze lifted the air, and yet the cloud moved towards them with great speed.

The two young men stood perfectly still. As the cloud got closer, they both saw that it was actually a beautiful woman who seemed to be floating across the plains. Her long, glistening hair streamed out behind her like a gentle breeze. She was dressed completely in white buckskin, and on her back she carried a bundle. The older brother was paralysed with awe. He could see that this mysterious woman was a holy spirit, and he waited for her message.

The younger brother, who saw only her beauty, fell instantly in love. 'This woman is meant for me,' he thought to himself. And he ran towards her. As soon as she saw this, the woman laid down her bundle and opened her arms. As she wrapped them around the young man, a cloud of white glistening dust rose up around them. The older brother waited, not taking his eyes from the cloud. A few minutes passed, and a soft wind blew the cloud apart. There was the beautiful woman standing alone. At her feet was a pile of bones.

'You are a wise man,' said the holy woman to the older brother, staring into his eyes. 'Go and tell your chief, Standing Hollow Horn, that I am coming. Tell him to make a lodge that is large enough to hold all his people. When everyone is gathered in the lodge, I will come.'

The young man bowed and went directly to Standing Hollow Horn's tipi. The chief listened and nodded. He knew, just as the older brother had,

that the mysterious woman was a holy spirit. The people dismantled their tipis so they would have enough skins and poles to make a large sacred lodge. When it was finished, all the children and women and men of the tribe gathered inside and waited. Great excitement filled their hearts.

'She is coming! I see the cloud!' called a young man. Indeed, the glowing white cloud was moving quickly over the plains towards the great sacred lodge.

When the mysterious woman entered the lodge, the people all saw what the older brother had seen. They saw a woman whose long flowing hair slid through the air like wind. They saw a woman whose wide, dark eyes shone with the kindness of the oldest grandmother. They saw a woman whose smile was full of wisdom and kindness. The people's hearts were full of love for this woman. Their hearts were full of awe.

They watched as she walked sun-wise round the lodge, from the south to the west to the north and finally to the east. They saw her stop before Standing Hollow Horn, who sat in the place of honour.

She took her bundle from her back and held it out towards the chief.

'Behold this and always love it,' she said. 'Inside this bundle is a sacred pipe, which I have brought to your people.'

Then she carefully untied the bundle with her long, graceful fingers. 'The Earth is your Mother and Grandmother,' she said. 'When you walk on the Earth, you are making a prayer to Her.' Then she lifted the pipe from the bundle and held it up for everyone to see. She showed the people the bowl of the pipe, which was made of red stone. She showed them the buffalo that was carved into the side of the bowl.

'The buffalo is the symbol of our Mother's four-legged children,' she said. 'The stem of the pipe, which is made of wood, is the symbol of Her green growing children.' From the stem of the pipe hung twelve feathers. 'These eagle feathers are the symbol of our winged brothers and sisters,' she said. 'We are all one family. When you smoke this pipe, you will make a prayer for the good of all of our Mother's children. When you pray with this pipe, all beings of the Universe will be a family.'

Then she took a red stone from her bundle and placed it upon the ground. She touched the stone on the ground with the bowl of the pipe. 'This stone is from our Mother's body, the Earth where we live. When the sun rises, remember that all two-legged children who stand on the Earth with you are your brothers and sisters. Treat every two-legged child with respect.' Then she gave the bundle and the pipe and the stone to Standing Hollow Horn.

She showed the people the seven circles which were carved into the stone, and she explained that each circle represents a sacred ceremony. 'Standing Hollow Horn,' she said, 'the Great Spirit gives you this pipe so you will have knowledge. I will teach you the first ceremony, and you will learn the others in time.'

Then she explained the sacred ceremony for keeping the soul of the dead close to the tribe. 'When someone dies, the person chosen to keep the soul of the dead will smoke the pipe. That person must be pure and good. On the day when the soul is released, four women will become sacred. And from these women will come children. In this way, your people will increase, and your people will be blessed.'

The people listened to the mysterious spirit woman. Everyone trusted her completely. 'I am the symbol of the four ages of time,' she said. 'I shall look back on your people from every age, and in the end I shall return.' Everyone wondered what she meant. Again, they watched her walk around the lodge in a sun-wise direction. Never taking their eyes from her, they watched as she walked out on to the plains.

Not far from the lodge, the holy woman stopped and looked back. She sat down on the ground. When she stood up a few moments later, the people were astonished. The beautiful woman with long flowing hair had turned into a red and brown buffalo calf.

The people stared as the young calf turned and walked on towards the horizon. After some distance, the calf lay down and rolled on her back.

Then she paused and looked back at the people, and when she stood up, her thick curly coat was as white as snow. No one took their eyes from the gleaming white buffalo as she walked on towards the horizon.

Again, after some distance, the buffalo paused and looked back at the people as she rolled on the ground. This time when she stood up, her thick curly coat had turned as black as the night. The people continued to stare as the black buffalo walked on for some time.

She was quite a distance from the people now, near the top of a long, sloping hill. She turned and looked at the people, and she bowed towards each of the four directions. Then, as the people all stared, she turned into tiny fragments of light. A gentle breeze blew over the plain, and she disappeared.

The people took care of the sacred pipe which was given to them by White Buffalo Woman. They taught their children the seven ceremonies. As time went on, the people understood that, by changing her colour, White Buffalo Woman was showing them the four ages of time. Each new era was heralded by the appearance of a special buffalo. In the late twentieth century, a white buffalo was born in the United States. People from all nations and tribes have gathered to see her. Her name is Miracle.

Cerridwen

WELSH

Cerridwen, whose name means 'White Grain', is also known as the White Goddess. She is a powerful magician who works her spells by mixing ingredients in a great copper cauldron. Cerridwen blesses poets and musicians with her spells. She is also a goddess of fertility, death and rebirth. This is the story of how Cerridwen gave birth to two sons, the second being Taliesin, one of the most famous bards of Celtic history. Later bards who composed funeral elegies called themselves 'cerddorion', or sons of Cerridwen.

MOTHER OF MAGIC

Long, long ago, on an island in the middle of Lake Tegid in the north of Wales, there lived a great magician known as Cerridwen. She spent her days brewing potions to bless the work of poets and musicians. She loved to talk to the animals, whose shapes she could take at will. Cerridwen enjoyed a life of beauty and ease on the island, until the day she gave birth to her son.

Cerridwen wrapped her baby in the folds of her long white gown. Her tears fell on to the tiny boy's misshapen body as she softly sang a lullaby. One of his legs was longer than the other. He would walk with a limp. His body was covered with coarse, dark hair, and the features of his face made him seem more like a beast than a boy.

As she sang, she thought about how much he would suffer with this ungraceful body. He would be ridiculed. He would never be welcomed in the High Court of the Land. She could reshape his body with magic, but magic would fade. There was really nothing she could do to change her son's sad appearance. Cerridwen sighed and decided to call him Great Crow, for he reminded her of that magical bird. She tucked the poor little thing into a sling close to her body, and set about searching her books for a spell that would somehow enrich his life.

At midnight, the moon's silver light slanted into the room, falling on one of the books Cerridwen had already looked through. She opened it again, and her eyes instantly fell upon the information she needed.

'Of course!' she sang, holding the baby up as she danced around the room. 'I will give you the most melodious voice ever heard. Birds will stop singing to hear your song. The finest musicians will sit at your side. And I will give you the gift of the Sight, my boy. Kings and magicians will stop talking to listen when you speak of the future! They will fight for your favour. Great battles will be won with your wisdom, my child!'

Cerridwen immediately wrote a list of the plants she would need to gather. Mugwort, shepherd's purse, sage, yarrow and more. The list was long. The plants she needed grew during different seasons and on different parts of the island. 'I will be gathering for a year and a day,' she said to the baby. 'I will be placing blossoms and leaves and seeds and roots into the cauldron right up until the day when the brew is ready for you, my son.'

The next morning, Cerridwen sang as she tucked Great Crow into his sling. She sang as she strode to the stream where the apple moss grew. Asking for the plant's blessing, she broke off what she needed and placed it into her pouch. Cerridwen hired an old man who was blind to stir the brew in the cauldron, and she hired a young boy named Gwion Bach to feed the fire. That evening she sang the 'Spell of Promise' to Great Crow as she rocked him to sleep.

In the morning, Gwion Bach laid a four-square fire with birchbark and hazel branches in the tall pine grove. With hope in her heart, Cerridwen filled her great cauldron with water from the lake. She lit the fire with a coal from her hearth and within minutes the brew was boiling.

Just before midday, Cerridwen sent Gwion to gather wood in the forest. While he was gone, she sprinkled the moss and some mugwort into the cauldron when the sun's light streamed straight down from

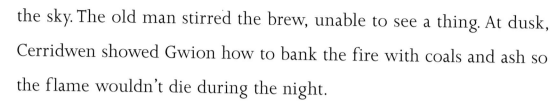

the sky. The old man stirred the brew, unable to see a thing. At dusk, Cerridwen showed Gwion how to bank the fire with coals and ash so the flame wouldn't die during the night.

The year passed with ritual regularity. Every day, Cerridwen gathered plants with prayer and added them to the boiling brew. In the heat of summer and the cold of winter, the old man stirred while the young boy tended the flame.

On the day that marked exactly one year's passing, Cerridwen held her son in her arms next to the cauldron.

'Tomorrow,' she sang into his little ear. 'Tomorrow you will be a new boy, my son!'

Gwion, who had just then returned from the forest, happened to hear Cerridwen's promise to her strange-looking son.

'Whatever could she mean?' he wondered. 'Whatever it is, I will be watching,' he thought to himself.

The next morning, as Gwion approached the tall pines, he was surprised not to find the old man stirring the brew, as he had every day for a year. Instead, Cerridwen was crouched on top of a boulder with her arms wrapped around her knees as she rocked back and forth. The night's coals had been brushed aside, and the fire flamed up the sides of the cauldron. These peculiar circumstances made Gwion uncomfortable, but he dared to look directly at Cerridwen. Her eyes were closed, and she was singing over and over: 'Now is the time, this is the day, now is the time, here is the change we're awaiting.' Then Gwion noticed the baby, Great Crow, sitting on a rock opposite his mother, quite close to the cauldron, which was glowing white-orange with heat.

A hissing sound whistled within the cauldron. Gwion boldly leaned over its lip to look inside. The sizzling brew had reduced to a minuscule amount, no more than four drops. Just then the brew reduced to three drops – the magical number – and the great cauldron cracked in two. Gwion stumbled and fell forward. One of his fingers dipped into the scorching hot brew. At once, he stuck his seared finger into his mouth to reduce the sting. In that instant Gwion Bach became the recipient of the gifts which were meant for Great Crow.

With the wisdom and foresight he had just received, the boy instantly knew how furious Cerridwen would be when she realised that her magic had blessed him and not her poor son. Without hesitating, Gwion turned himself into a strong-legged hare and bolted into the forest.

Cerridwen awoke from her trance and let out a cry of rage. She instantly turned herself into a sleek, black greyhound, bounding through the forest after Gwion. Hearing the greyhound crashing behind him, getting closer and closer, Gwion leaped into a stream, and turned himself into a fish flashing through the water. Cerridwen turned herself into an otter whooshing through the water straight after the fish. Gwion felt a nipping at his tail and he turned himself into a sparrow, soaring skywards.

Cerridwen turned herself into a hawk, speeding after the sparrow. 'What luck!' thought Gwion, as he darted through a knothole into a barn. Flinging himself at a bin of white corn, he turned himself into a kernel of corn and hid. Cerridwen turned herself into a red-legged, black hen, and she began to eat the entire bin of corn. When the last kernel had been eaten, Cerridwen again took the shape of a woman.

As she walked back to her cottage, full of despair for Great Crow, she felt the unmistakable stirring of new life inside her body. Indeed, Gwion Bach was growing into a child within her. Nine months passed, and Cerridwen gave birth to her second son. She held his tiny hand in hers and looked into his blue eyes. In her heart, she couldn't consider harming this child. Nor could she keep him, for he had, after all, stolen her first son's gifts. She wrapped the baby in her shawl and placed him into a cradle boat, which she launched into the lake.

The child was found by a heretofore-unlucky prince. As soon as the prince uncovered the baby, he saw a bright glow

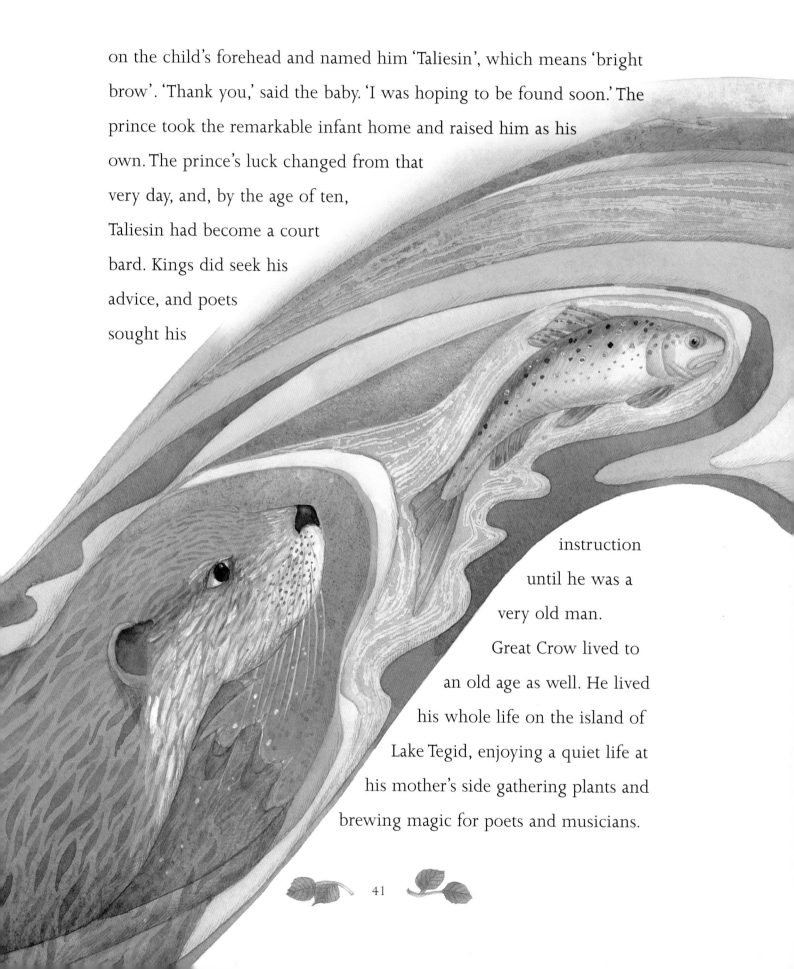

on the child's forehead and named him 'Taliesin', which means 'bright brow'. 'Thank you,' said the baby. 'I was hoping to be found soon.' The prince took the remarkable infant home and raised him as his own. The prince's luck changed from that very day, and, by the age of ten, Taliesin had become a court bard. Kings did seek his advice, and poets sought his instruction until he was a very old man. Great Crow lived to an old age as well. He lived his whole life on the island of Lake Tegid, enjoying a quiet life at his mother's side gathering plants and brewing magic for poets and musicians.

41

Freya

SCANDINAVIAN

Freya, whose name means 'Lady' or 'Mistress', is the northern European goddess of love, desire, sorcery and magic. She is also a goddess of war and of death. After every battle, Freya and Odin enter the battlefield to collect the souls of the dead. Those who are fortunate enough to be chosen by Freya are taken to her palace in the Other World where they are treated to feasting and festivity, music, art and love. This story is about how Freya uses her magical power to achieve her heart's desire.

THE BLESSING NECKLACE

Long, long ago, in the court of Odin the Terrible, there was a goddess named Freya whose beauty was exceptionally rare. Her hair streamed down her back like a sheath of shimmering gold and her eyes were the same brilliant blue as the sky. She walked with the grace of a dancer. Freya was so fond of adorning herself that she had ten rooms full of gowns and cloaks and six rooms full of shoes and boots. She especially loved jewellery.

One winter night, as she lay asleep in her palace, Freya dreamed of an ancient ash tree. A mysterious web of light sparkled like diamonds all over one side of its wide, furrowed bark. Freya awoke from her dream and pulled her quilt up over her shoulders.

'I know where that tree is!' she exclaimed out loud. 'I know exactly where that tree is! And I want to know why that tree was in my dream,' she said, as she sat on the edge of her bed.

She pulled on her red fur-lined boots. She put on her falcon cloak. And she slid her hands into her long, black gloves as she strode through the halls of her palace. Freya leaped up the tower stairs. There, on the balcony under the light of the stars, she lifted into the cold, night air and swooped down towards Earth in search of the tree.

There it was – exactly where she thought it would be – standing tall in one of the sacred groves. Slipping off her glove, Freya slid her hand over its bumpy bark where she had seen the web of light. And as she had hoped, the tree split open for her, revealing a tunnel leading down into the Earth.

Freya thought she could hear distant singing and the rhythmic, sharp clang of a hammer. Her passion for music and mystery pulled on her heart and she quickly climbed into the tree.

Freya followed the tunnel down and down until she came at last to a brightly-lit chamber. Hesitating in the shadows, she saw four dwarfs crafting the most magnificent necklace she had ever seen. Many strands of delicate diamonds hung from several gold chains. Their light flickered and danced on the walls of the cave like the twinkling of the Milky Way. Freya's hand reached up to her throat, and she sighed with desire.

'Whoever wears that necklace wears the blessing of the Earth and the Sky,' she thought to herself, as her heart swelled with longing.

'Oh ho!' said Dvalin to Alfrigg as he hammered the gold. 'Someone's beauty is brightening our cave.'

'Indeed,' said Berling to Grerr as he cut the diamonds. 'Someone's desire is filling our cave.'

'If it gets any larger,' said Alfrigg to Grerr, 'our hearts will be squeezed into dust, and we'll be forced to halt the work at hand.'

'Kind sirs,' said the goddess, stepping forward. 'Please forgive my intrusion. I am Freya, Mistress of the Lovely Arts.' The four little men put down their tools as Freya bowed. Dvalin, the boldest, offered his arm as she rose.

'You clever men are the masters of your craft,' said Freya. 'If this treasure of light is for sale, I will give you gold and silver. I will give you eternal youth and joy everlasting. I will be honoured to wear the craft of your hand – these special jewels.'

Now, as you might imagine, the four dwarfs were completely astonished. Underworld dwarfs work for years at a time without receiving a guest. Berling, who was the most nervous, coughed and shuffled his feet. Then Alfrigg, who handled all business affairs, cleared his throat and spoke.

'My Lady, you can see we have all the riches we need. The Earth gives us long veins of gold and full mines of jewels. We are older than the stars and, as you can tell from our song, our hearts brim over with love for our work. We have no need of such things.'

Freya's heart tightened with sadness. What else could she offer?

'There is one thing we could accept in exchange for this circle of light, my Lady,' said Alfrigg.

'Yes? What is it?' Freya cried excitedly, without a second thought. 'Whatever it is, it is yours!'

Now Dvalin, the most handsome of the four, took Freya's hand and smiled into her eager eyes. 'Your company, Lady,' he replied. 'If you will kindly consent to remain with us while we finish the necklace, in four days' time it will rest forever on your elegant neck. Beauty belongs with beauty, my Lady.'

Freya's smile spread across her face like the sun rising over the ocean. 'Of course, of course, gentlemen. I will be honoured to be your guest.' The four little men bowed. As they rose, Freya hugged each one. And the party of four days and four nights began.

While Alfrigg continued to work on the necklace, Dvalin played the flute. Grerr took the lady's hand in dance. And Berling began to cook a feast. Freya danced with each little man. They sang every song they knew. And during the evenings, when they were tired, Freya told them stories that made them laugh until their faces hurt.

Meanwhile, up in the ash tree above the dwarfs's cave, someone was waiting for Freya to reappear. It was Odin, disguised as a wood rat. For four days and nights he had tried to gain entry to the sacred tree. By the fourth night, his curiosity had grown into an angry rant. 'What is she doing inside a tree for four days and nights?' he fumed.

Just at that moment, Dvalin added the clasp to the glistening necklace and fastened it around Freya's neck. Freya glowed with pleasure and the satisfaction that comes from fulfilling one's heart's desire.

Odin heard their voices getting louder, and he crouched in a shadow. As the tree split open, the light of the blessing necklace blinded his little rat eyes. Odin squinted them down to a slit, and he saw Freya hug and kiss each of the dwarfs. He saw the magnificent, dazzling necklace that lit up her throat. And he was so furious that he sat in that shadow for some time after Freya had flown off into the sky. Then he realised he was staring at a perfectly still black squirrel, who was staring at him. The squirrel suddenly sneezed with the sound of a man's sneeze. And Odin knew straight away that the squirrel was Loki, Freya's assistant, spying on him.

'Did you see that?' Odin said. 'Freya has persuaded those dwarfs to give her their magical handiwork. I want you to bring it to me.'

Loki chortled. 'Im-possible. My Lady wears it around her neck.'

Odin shifted back into the shape of a man and grabbed Loki's little squirrel neck. 'I will serve you to my wolves for breakfast if I do not have that necklace by dawn,' threatened Odin.

Poor Loki – what choice did he have? Returning to the palace, he took the shape of a dust mote and waited for the first breeze to blow him under the door of her bedchamber.

Once Loki was inside Freya's room, he took the shape of a flea. Leaping up on to her bed, he found her sound asleep with the blessing necklace still clasped around her neck. He hopped over her head, searching for the sleek gold clasp, which at last he realised was beneath her neck, quite out of reach. Loki scratched his little head. Then he opened his minuscule jaws over the goddess's shoulder and bit into her soft skin. Just as he'd hoped, Freya turned on to her side without waking. Then, resuming his own shape, Loki unfastened the necklace and dropped it into his pocket. He smiled as he boldly walked out of Freya's palace, leaving every door unlocked and wide open behind him.

It was mid-afternoon when Freya awoke. She reached for her necklace and, finding it gone, sprang to her feet in a fury. Only Loki could have gained entry into her palace. Only Odin could have set Loki against her. Freya slid her falcon cloak over her shoulders and winged her way to Odin's castle.

'I want my necklace,' demanded the goddess, waving her hand at Odin's wolves, who yawned and dropped to the floor in a deep sleep.

Odin didn't care. 'This necklace shines like the stars,' he smirked, sliding the diamond strands through his fingers.

'I want my necklace,' Freya repeated.

'This gold was crafted by artisan dwarfs. Its diamonds were cut by a master,' said Odin. 'Yes, indeed, this is a rare treasure. And I will give you your necklace, dear Freya. You may wear it forever, if you will give something to me.'

Freya sighed. 'You want me to make a battle for you, is that it?'

'Yes, of course,' he replied. 'But not just any battle. I want deep hatred. I want a battle between two Earthly kings whose legions of soldiers will fill the horizon. Pour fury into the hearts of the captains and their men and make them fight to the end. Let me see them all dying and dead on the fields. And then, in exchange for your necklace of stars, revive each of the dead. Heal them so they stand strong and hearty and full of hatred again. Give me two roaring rounds of battle, my Lady, and then I will give you this string of stars that you so desire.'

Freya stepped back. She gazed out through the window for a moment, and then she turned towards Odin. 'I will give you two rounds of battle between two Earthly kings and their armies,' she replied, 'and I will do that for you as soon as you give me my necklace.'

Odin handed Freya her necklace, which she immediately fastened around her throat. Its light sparkled all over the room, dazzling Odin so that he flinched and squinted, shielding his eyes with his hand. Freya walked over to Odin's balcony. She lifted her arms, her cloak draping down like great wings. Then she rose into the air and flew down through the clouds to Earth. It was time to begin her search for two hot-headed kings.

Ama-terasu

JAPANESE

Ama-terasu, whose name means 'Shining in Heaven', is the Shinto goddess of the sun. She is the ruler of the six directions: North, East, South and West, the Great Above and the Great Below. Still worshipped in Japan today, Ama-terasu is considered the Ancestral Mother of the Japanese people. This story, which begins with the explanation of her birth, is about how she once disappeared, leaving Heaven and Earth in darkness.

AMA-TERASU'S MIRROR

Long, long ago, before anything we know existed, the first deities were born in the Heavens. The first goddess, She-Who-Invites, and her husband, He-Who-Invites, stood on the floating bridge that stretched from Heaven to Earth, and together they created the islands of Japan.

Then She-Who-Invites gave birth to the gods and goddesses who ruled over Earth's mountains, streams and lakes. The last was a fire god, whose scorching heat burned She-Who-Invites so severely that she died. He-Who-Invites fell down at his wife's side and held her as he cried rivers of tears. He-Who-Invites cried for weeks. At last, a girl child was born from his eye, who glowed so brightly and who was so pleasant to look at that He-Who-Invites stopped crying to rejoice.

'Your light is so bright that I will call you Ama-terasu,' proclaimed He-Who-Invites. 'You will rule over the High Plain of Heaven, my child.'

He-Who-Invites was so pleased by the birth of his beautiful daughter that he immediately slipped his precious necklace of glistening jewels over his head and placed it around her neck.

Then from the nose of He-Who-Invites, a boy child was born – a boy who wriggled and rolled from side to side. As soon as he stood, he hopped back and forth from one foot to the other until he finally broke into a run, dashing round and round his father and sister in great excitement. 'You I will call Susa-no, Brave-and-Swift-Impetuous-One,' said He-Who-Invites. 'You will rule over the world below. You will rule over all of Earth's land and seas, my son.'

Ama-terasu immediately took charge of the sky, but Susa-no did not move an inch to take charge of Earth's land and seas. This boy was so sad when he heard about his mother's death, he was unable to do a thing. Susa-no sulked for so long that Earth's seas dried up from neglect. Forests became deserts, and Earth's lush greenery withered and shrivelled.

He-Who-Invites was furious with Susa-no for not taking care of the Earth's land and seas. He banished Susa-no from his divine home on the High Plain of Heaven for not fulfilling his responsibility.

'Father, I beg you,' pleaded Susa-no, 'before I take my leave, allow me to say farewell to my illustrious sister, Ama-terasu. Before I leave, let me see her once more.'

He-Who-Invites nodded, and Susa-no rose up to Heaven. Below him, Earth's mountains and rivers shook and rumbled, roaring a warning to Ama-terasu in the High Plain of Heaven.

'My brother, Brave-and-Swift-Impetuous-One, is coming this way,' she said to herself. 'He will try to take my lands for himself now that he has been banished.'

Ama-terasu twisted her hair into two round buns, tucked them inside her head-dress, and covered her arms with chains of glittering jewels. She slung a quiver of five hundred arrows over her shoulder. Holding on to her bow, she stood on the crest of a cloud, watching Susa-no rise higher into the sky. She stamped her foot as he faced her, and a great wide wind blew forth.

'What brings you here, Brother?' she demanded.

'I have come to bid you farewell, illustrious Ama-terasu. I have come to pay my respects before I leave the Heavens forever.'

Then Susa-no went on to tell Ama-terasu how much he loved her and how much he would miss her. But this was not really true. In his heart, Susa-no was jealous of his glorious sister whose great light brightened all of Heaven and Earth.

'To prove that I come of good heart, let us both give birth to children.
I will show you that my intentions are good by giving birth to boys
while you give birth to girls,' proposed Susa-no.

Ama-terasu nodded in agreement. From her breath, she gave birth
to several girl deities, and from his breath Susa-no gave birth to several
boys. Excited with his success, Susa-no began to jump up and down,
flailing his arms in a wild dance of victory. As usual, his excitement
grew like a stream rushing towards a waterfall. Susa-no ran through
the rice fields crying out in a booming voice, 'I have shown my sister
that I mean her no harm! I have shown my sister my sons!'

Susa-no didn't seem to notice that he was breaking the walls that
separate the heavenly rice fields as he ran swiftly through them. He
didn't seem to notice that he was filling the irrigation ditches with the
earth he kicked up. He didn't even seem to notice when he knocked over

the tables that Ama-terasu had set for the Celebration of the First Fruits.

'My brother is still a wild child,' Ama-terasu thought to herself. 'After a while, he will calm down.' She removed her warrior head-dress and her quiver, put down her bow, and joined the women in the sacred Weaving Hall. As she sat weaving, her brother Susa-no, the Brave-and-Swift-Impetuous-One, continued to run wildly over her lands, destroying whatever was in his path.

When Susa-no realised that Ama-terasu seemed to be ignoring him, his brow creased and his excitement turned to anger. 'I will make my sister see how powerful I am,' he decided.

Susa-no launched a long metal pole at the roof of the sacred Weaving Hall. The roof shattered and split open. The women inside screamed as the mighty pole flew through the air, striking Ama-terasu's own shuttle, splitting it in two.

'My father was right to banish this man. Susa-no has no intention of behaving as he should,' she cried, as she fled from the Weaving Hall. 'I will not let him see me again,' she said to herself as she ran straight to the Sky-Rock-Cave, bolting its entrance behind her.

Of course, darkness immediately fell over the High Plain of Heaven and all over the Earth. The gods and goddesses groped for their lanterns. And with that dim, soft light, they made their way to the Tranquil River where all eight hundred of them assembled. There a god called Everyone's-Thoughts made a plan.

The night birds sang while the gods and goddesses dragged rocks from the Tranquil River. Iron was brought from the Heavenly Metal-Mountains. In that eternal night, by the light of lanterns, the old smith goddess named One-Eye set up a forge outside the Sky-Rock-Cave. She built a fire and melted the river rock and the iron and shaped it into a beautiful mirror. Then with her own shawl old One-Eye polished the mirror until it was as smooth as the surface of the river itself. The oldest cherry tree was uprooted and replanted near the entrance to the Sky-Rock-Cave, and the great Sky-Mirror was carefully placed in its branches, which were decorated with long cloth streamers and strings of jewels. The gods placed the softest white and blue cloths under the tree as offerings for Ama-terasu. And they all began to recite ritual words for her return.

Just then, the goddess Izume-the-Alarming-One dragged a heavy metal tub to the entrance to the cave. As the tub scraped across the rocky ground it made a loud shrieking cry, which caused the gods to cover their ears.

'Whatever could that screech be?' wondered Ama-terasu.

Izume-the-Alarming-One turned over the metal tub. She climbed on top of it and began to stamp her feet as she danced and sang, waving her sash above her head. She squatted down and made herself small, and she squeezed her face into a puckered prune. She jumped up and down and stretched her face so her mouth was a wide cavern. Izume stood on her head. She stood on her elbows. She crossed her arms and legs and tied her body into a knot. All eight hundred gods and goddesses began to laugh.

Each time Izume did something new with her body, they laughed louder and louder until their delight began to rumble like thunder.

'What can be going on out there in the dark?' thought Ama-terasu. The entire High Plain of Heaven shook with the laughter of the gods and goddesses. Ama-terasu was curious, but she still did not come out of the Sky-Rock-Cave.

Izume lifted the cloth from a cage which held twelve cocks that crow before dawn. The birds thought the removal of the cloth was their cue to crow, which they immediately did to greet the day.

'Why are cocks crowing when there is no sun in the High Plain of Heaven?' said Ama-terasu out loud. Now her curiosity was too great to contain. She leaned against the bolt of the entrance to the cave and pushed the door open. From inside Ama-terasu called out, 'What goes on out there? What makes you people so pleased that you laugh with delight when I have taken away the light?'

'We are celebrating, Ama-terasu,' called out Izume. 'We are celebrating the arrival of a sun goddess whose brightness is as brilliant as yours!'

'I must meet this goddess!' insisted Ama-terasu as she began pushing open the door. As she did so, the gods tilted the mirror so it completely reflected her image. Brightness flooded the High Plain of Heaven, streaming in long glowing rays down to Earth and beyond.

Immediately the god Heavenly-Hand-Strength took Ama-terasu's hand and led her out of the cave towards the mirror. No one in those times

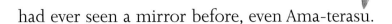

had ever seen a mirror before, even Ama-terasu. When she realised that she was looking at her own reflection, she laughed. All eight hundred deities cheered her name.

Everyone's-Thoughts stepped forward. 'We have missed your bright warmth, Honourable Ama-terasu. Without you, there is no joy in the High Plain of Heaven. Without your far-reaching rays, nothing grows on Earth. Please do not go into the Sky-Rock-Cave again.'

Ama-terasu nodded. 'You can be sure I will never hide my light from the world again,' she said as she ran her hand over the mirror. Then she bowed to the goddesses and gods. 'This shining surface that multiplies sunlight is sacred,' she said. 'Adore this sky-mirror as you adore your own soul.'

The eight hundred goddesses and gods fined Susa-no an enormous amount of money for the damage he had caused, and they cut off his beard before they banished him from the High Plain of Heaven. Ama-terasu eventually sent the Sky-Mirror to Earth where it is still kept in the shrine which was built in her honour.

Oshun

NIGERIAN – YORUBA

Oshun, whose name means 'The Source', has been worshipped as the Mother of the Yoruba people for thousands of years. She is a wealthy and beautiful goddess who rules over many aspects of life, but especially love and beauty. Oshun likes to adorn herself with fine clothing. She uses her powers to bring children to couples who have none. She is a fierce protectress of everything she nourishes. This is the story of how Oshun bargained with the gods as they prepared the Earth for the first humans and of how she gave birth to these first humans.

THE GREAT MOTHER

Before the beginning of time, Olodumare, the Supreme Sky Being, looked down at Earth. He gazed at the reflection of the stars twinkling on the surface of Earth's vast waters. He watched the sunlight blazing bright red over the mountains. 'Earth is so beautiful,' Olodumare said to himself. 'I will now populate the Earth with human beings to take care of Her.' Olodumare called seventeen gods to prepare Earth for human life. And he called one goddess, Oshun.

'Find the right place on Earth for the first people,' said Olodumare. 'Make sure they will have what they need. Make sure Earth is ready for human beings.'

The gods were excited. They immediately began to hold meetings

to discuss what needed to be done. Earth was still a young planet. The ground rumbled and shook and split open in wide jagged gaps. Wild winds blew over the seas, lifting the water in great gusts, flooding the land. Volcanic lava poured down mountain slopes and white flakes of ash fell from the sky.

The gods loved solving problems like this. They set about their task with great pleasure. Being gods, they all understood the importance of creating harmony and keeping everything in balance. They were so excited by their task, however, it never occurred to any of them to invite Oshun to their meetings. Even when they went down to Earth to harness the powerful forces of nature, they did not think of inviting Oshun.

Oshun put on her deep purple robe. She sat down at her dressing table to braid her hair. She knew the men had forgotten about her. 'Such foolishness,' she said to herself, and she sighed. Oshun tied red and yellow beads to her braids. She tucked a turquoise feather behind her ear. And she made a plan.

Down on Earth, the gods were moving a river so it would flow into the sea. Ogun and Orunmila held the banks of one side and Eshu and Jakuta held the other.

'Lift!' cried Ogun, and the gods pulled the river up out of its bed. It rippled like a long satin

ribbon as it slid out of their hands, gushing back on to the ground. Three times Ogun cried 'Lift!' and three times the river slipped out of their hands. No matter how hard they tried, the gods were unable to move the river.

The same thing happened when they tried to close the volcanoes. In fact, none of their plans to prepare Earth for humanity worked. There was nothing to do but report this sad truth to Olodumare, who listened patiently as the gods described their thwarted efforts.

'Where is Oshun?' asked Olodumare. 'Did her efforts fail as well?'

'We did not invite a woman to our planning meetings, Olodumare,' said Eshu. 'What could a woman do to help with our work?'

'You have upset the balance,' said Olodumare. 'A team of men cannot create harmony on Earth without a woman. Without Oshun, no plan will unfold. She has the power to undo each action you make. Clearly, this is what she is doing. If Earth's mighty lands will be tamed and her oceans contained, you must work with Oshun as I instructed.'

The gods nodded. They knew they had made a mistake. They brought Oshun fragrant soaps and oils. They brought her kola nuts, brilliant blue feathers for her hair and many brass bracelets, which she immediately slid on to her arms.

Oshun smiled at the gods.

'You are wise to restore

the balance by

coming to me. I see you have brought me the things I love.'

'Forgive us,' pleaded Orunmila. 'We were so eager to create balance for the humans on Earth, we forgot about keeping the balance between us. Please look in your heart for forgiveness.'

'I will forgive you, of course.' replied Oshun. 'And together we will make Earth ready for humans. But first, there is something you must do for me.'

'Anything, whatever you wish,' said Sango, who was eager to get back to work. The other gods nodded in agreement.

'I want you to tell me the secrets of the Universe. I want you to show me how to see the future in the cowrie shells.'

The gods stepped back. Their eyebrows arched over their eyes. No one but a man knew the secrets of the cowrie shells. The gods were shocked to hear a woman even ask for this knowledge. Some of the gods were angry, but they all knew they would have to fulfil Oshun's request in order to restore the balance.

Eshu stepped forward and pulled a pouch from his pocket. As he untied the pouch, he looked at each of the gods. 'We men have held the secrets of the Universe for aeons,' he said. 'Now we must share the power of the cowrie shells with the women.'

Orunmila and the other gods nodded. Eshu shook the cowrie shells in his hands. He blew on the shells. Then he threw them on to the ground. Orunmila showed Oshun how to understand the pattern the shells made

when they landed, sometimes a circle, sometimes a line. He showed her what it meant when the slit in the shell was facing upwards and what it meant when the slit faced the ground. He taught her the songs to be sung with each pattern. Oshun learned quickly. Soon she could tell what the future would bring by looking at the shells. Oshun smiled and rubbed her belly with delight.

'Now, let's get to work!' she suggested.

All seventeen gods and Oshun returned to Earth. 'We must make sure that there are wide grassy fields for the animals. Humans will need good hunting grounds,' said Jakuta. 'And clear, clean water for drinking and bathing,' said Oshun. Rivers were redirected. Volcanoes were closed. Earth stopped trembling. The gods planted fields of grain and orchards of fruit-bearing trees.

When everything was in order, Oshun squatted next to a cold, rushing river. The sound of the water soothed her to sleep. After some time, her brass bracelets began to jangle and her big, round body began to shake. The gods watched at a distance, each amazed by the calm expression

on Oshun's face as she gave birth to the first people. One after another, fully formed miniature men and women emerged from her body.

'She gives birth with the ease of a sunrise!' said Orunmila.

'She gives birth with the ease of an opening flower!' said Ogun.

Oshun held each of the first people in her arms. She blessed each one with a prayer of prosperity and sent them off to make homes and villages. The gods watched in amazement at her tenderness and love.

Their work was complete. The gods and goddess returned to the sky and Oshun continued to watch over her children. She smiled as she saw them discovering how to use corn for food. She smiled when the people discovered fire. She was pleased when they taught their children songs about her and called her their Mother.

Oshun taught the first women how to weave cloth and how to dye it bright colours with the juice squeezed from berries. She taught them how to cook fritters. She showed them how to throw the cowrie shells so they could see the future. She watched as the women played with their children, and she laughed out loud when she saw them splashing in the river with the fish.

Oshun began to long for a child of her own. She drank from the nourishing waters of the river each day, just as the women on Earth did, but no child grew within her body. Oshun prayed for a child of her own every night, but even so, no child grew within her. She continued to watch over Earth's children, longing for one of her own.

One day, Oshun heard a woman teaching her children about the importance of keeping all things in balance. The woman told her children the story about the gods who forgot to include Oshun as they prepared Earth for the first people. 'How could the gods forget Mother Oshun?' demanded the children. 'How did she ever forgive them?'

'They had to give up something they loved,' said the woman. 'They had to give up holding the secrets of the cowrie shells to restore the balance.'

When Oshun heard this, she realised what she needed to do. More than anything, she enjoyed adorning herself with fancy, bright robes and feathers. It gave her great pleasure to anoint her skin and her hair with rich oils to make it soft. Oshun treasured her collection of combs

and her bracelets. 'None of these beautiful things can compare to the joy of a child,' she said, as she packed them into baskets and chests.

Oshun gave away all her brightly coloured robes, and she gave away her combs and her bracelets and beads. Indeed, after some time of living quite plainly, just as the women on Earth did, Oshun gave birth to her own child. Soon after that, she gave birth to another. And so it went until Oshun had many children. There was never a mother who enjoyed her children more than Oshun – cooking for them and dyeing the cloth for their clothing, pounding the corn and teaching her children all the songs she knew. When Oshun's children were grown and they realised what their mother had sacrificed, they replenished her wealth and brought her fine robes and brass bracelets to restore the balance.

The Triple Goddess

GREEK

Persephone, Demeter and Hekate represent the daughter, mother and grandmother, but together they are often thought of as one goddess, which is why they are referred to as the Triple Goddess. Persephone, the young girl, rules over spring; Demeter, her mother, the mature woman, rules over the summer. Hekate, the old woman, rules over winter. This is the story of how Persephone became Queen of the Underworld and of Demeter and Hekate's devotion to her.

PERSEPHONE, DEMETER AND HEKATE

In ancient times, there was a goddess named Demeter who blessed the seeds beneath the soil, bringing forth all green growing plants. During the first warm days of spring, Demeter strode with her daughter, Persephone, over the Earth singing ritual songs to open the seeds and make them grow. In midsummer and autumn, when the people joyfully harvested bountiful crops, they sang praise to Demeter. Many seasons passed pleasantly as Persephone grew from a child into a young woman, until one glorious summer afternoon.

On that day, Persephone and her cousins had gathered in a field of brilliant flowers. After playing several games, they lay down in a circle

with their heads together. A warm, gentle breeze blew through the field and quietness fell over that place. As her cousins began to fall asleep, Persephone noticed the scent of narcissi in the air. 'How peculiar,' she thought. 'This is not the season for narcissi.' Knowing that her mother would want to know about such an unusual occurrence, Persephone followed the scent across the field.

Indeed, over the low hill at the far end of the field, she found a narcissus in full bloom. But this was no ordinary narcissus. This narcissus had one hundred blossoms all oozing out a powerfully sweet perfume. Persephone reached out to touch it and the Earth began to tremble beneath her feet. She lost her balance and toppled over as the field split in two, completely separating her from her cousins. Six enormous black stallions clambered out of the chasm, drawing the gleaming gold chariot of Hades, Lord of the Underworld. 'My beauty!' Hades called as he reined in the snorting black beasts. 'My beauty! My beloved! I've come to take you for my wife!'

The mighty Hades, whose purple hair streamed out behind him, bent down, grabbed hold of Persephone's waist and pulled her into his chariot. She screamed for help but the thundering horses' hooves muffled the sound of her voice, and none of her cousins heard her cry.

Fortunately, Old Hekate happened to be standing nearby in the mouth of her cave on the edge of the field. 'What goes on here?' she wondered, as she felt the Earth tremble and moan. 'Who cries for help in this peaceful place?' she asked, as she hobbled into the field. Hekate heard the powerful stampeding horses and watched as they drew the gold chariot over the field towards Hades's cave. 'That wicked Hades!' said Hekate, shaking her staff. 'He's up to no good.'

Demeter also heard Persephone's screams. She ran from her temple all the way to the field, but, by the time she arrived, there was no sign of her daughter. Hades's chariot had disappeared. 'My daughter, my daughter,' Demeter cried. 'Where is my daughter?' she wailed, swiftly swooping all over Earth in search of her dear Persephone. Ten days later, Hekate found Demeter wandering in the field, wearing a long black cloak and wringing her hands. Tears streamed down her cheeks. 'Where can she be? Where can my daughter be?' she said again and again.

'Demeter,' said Hekate, placing her arm around Demeter's waist. 'I felt the Earth tremble. I heard the field open, and I heard a young maiden cry out. Then I saw Hades's snorting black horses drawing his chariot, speeding through the field back to his cave. We must ask the

Sun, who sees everything and everyone on Earth, what he saw that day.'

'Hades did this, it is true,' said the Sun when they consulted him. 'He took Persephone and Zeus blessed their marriage.'

Demeter's jaw dropped open and her eyes widened in disbelief. 'Zeus blessed their marriage?' she repeated, her heart swelling with rage. 'How dare Zeus do such a thing without my consent?'

Demeter refused to go to Zeus's assembly on Mount Olympus. She was so angry and sad, she refused to bless the seeds and bring forth the crops on Earth. Grapes withered on the vine, and the olive trees dropped their leaves. In the spring no green shoots poked through the soil, and there were no crops to harvest. The people began to run out of food.

Hekate called on Zeus in his great palace on top of Mount Olympus. 'If Demeter does not bless the seeds,' said Hekate, 'there will be no food for the animals or for the humans. Earth's people will perish. Think about it, Zeus,' she said, leaning on her staff. 'If there are no humans on Earth, who will worship you or the rest of your gods?'

Zeus pulled on his beard. 'You are right,' he replied. Then Zeus sent the goddess Iris to plead with Demeter, who replied to her, 'I will not bless anything until I see my daughter again!'

Zeus finally sent Hermes to call on Hades in the Underworld. Hermes saw how thin and pale Persephone had become. Her eyes were filled with tears. 'Lord Hades,' he said. 'I come on behalf of my father, who has commanded me to lead Persephone out of this place. Demeter has

refused to bless the crops since the day of your marriage. Earth's fields are bare. The people are running out of food. Zeus has no option. He must make peace with Demeter.'

Hades wrung his hands. He slowly turned towards his queen. 'You may go to your stubborn mother,' he whispered. 'You may go to perform the rituals, blessing Earth's crops. But…' Then he paused, holding his palm out to his wife. 'You must eat these pomegranate seeds before you go.'

Persephone furrowed her brow and looked directly into Hades's red eyes. 'If I eat these seeds,' she said, 'I will be bound to return to this place.'

Hades smiled. 'You are right, my wise wife,' he replied. 'If you eat these six seeds you must return to me for six months every year. The rest of the year you will be free to bless the crops with your mother.'

Persephone considered Hades's offer. Glee spread through her body as she thought about seeing her mother again. If she ate the seeds, she could also continue to rule over the dead, who needed a queen, for half of the year. Persephone nodded and swallowed the seeds. Hades harnessed his huge black horses to his golden chariot, and handed a whip to Hermes. The horses charged through the hall and up the long tunnel to Earth's surface, flying over mountains and rivers to Demeter's temple.

When Demeter saw the chariot land, she leaped to her feet and ran to embrace Persephone. She and Hekate listened to her stories about Hades and the Underworld and the seeds she had eaten. 'I will reside with you for half the year, Mother. Together we will sing the ritual songs to bless the seeds, and together we shall celebrate the bountiful harvests. In the autumn, when the vines wither and die, I will rejoin my husband and be a guide to the dead. Then when the frosts give way to the warm sunlight of spring, I will return to you again.'

Hekate rested her hands on Demeter and Persephone's shoulders. 'You have struck a wise compromise, Persephone. Earth will flourish, and the people will sing praise to Demeter again. Every autumn, when you return to the land of the dead, I will go with you.'

'Grandmother Hekate, I gladly accept your offer,' said Persephone. Each year when she returned to the Underworld, Persephone rode through the withering fields with Hekate in Hades's gleaming gold chariot. While they were gone, winter fell upon the land, and the fields rested. Then, when the warm sunlight of spring brought the farmers to the fields to plant their seeds, Persephone and Hekate returned to Olympus. Demeter and Persephone blessed the seeds and the three goddesses celebrated with enormous feasts of fruit and great garlands of flowers.

Sources

Badejo, Diedre, *Osun Seegesi, The Elegant Deity of Wealth, Power and Femininity*, Africa World Press, Trenton, New Jersey, 1996.

Bascom, William, *Sixteen Cowries, Yoruba Divination from Africa to the New World*, Indiana University Press, Bloomington, Indiana and London, 1980.

Bell, Robert E., *Women of Classical Mythology*, Oxford University Press, Oxford and New York, 1991.

Bierhorst, John, *The Mythology of South America*, William Morrow, New York, 1988.

Bonheim, Jalaja, *Goddess: A Celebration in Art and Literature*, Stewart, Tabori & Chang, New York, 1996.

Brown, Joseph Eppes, *The Sacred Pipe*, Penguin Books, London and New York, 1971.

Carlyon, Richard, *A Guide to the Gods*, William Morrow, New York, 1981.

Chamberlain, Basil Hall, *Translation of Ko-Ji-Ki or Records of Ancient Matters*, J. L. Thompson & Co, Ltd, Kobe, Japan, 1932.

Colum, Padraic, 'The Children of Odin' from *The Book of Norse Myths*, The Macmillan Company, London and New York, 1962.

Cott, Jonathan, *Isis and Osiris*, Doubleday, New York, 1994.

Crossley-Holland, Kevin, *The Norse Myths*, Pantheon Books, New York, 1980.

Ford, Patrick K., *The Mabinogion and Other Medieval Welsh Tales*, University of California Press, Berkeley, Los Angeles and London, 1977.

Gottner-Abendroth, Heide, *The Goddess and Her Heroes*, Anthony Publishing Company, Stow, Massachusetts, 1995.

Graves, Robert, *The White Goddess*, Farrar, Straus & Giroux, New York, 1948.

Guirand, Felix, ed., *Larousse Encyclopedia of Mythology*, Paul Hamlyn, London, 1952.

Hutton, Ronald, *The Pagan Religions of the Ancient British Isles*, Blackwells, Oxford and Cambridge, Massachusetts, 1991.

Karade, Baba Ifa, *The Handbook of Yoruba Religious Concepts*, Samuel Weiser, Inc., York Beach, Maine, 1994.

Keightley, Thomas, *The Mythology of Ancient Greece and Italy*, Whitaker & Co, London, 1838.

Kinsley, David, *The Goddesses' Mirror*, State University of New York Press, Albany, New York, 1989.

Leeming, David and Page, Jake, *Goddess, Myths of the Female Divine*, Oxford University Press, Oxford and New York, 1994.

Lurker, Manfred, *Dictionary of Gods and Goddesses, Devils and Demons*, Routledge, London and New York, 1988.

MacCulloch, J. A., *Celtic Mythology*, Dorset Press, New York, 1992.

MacCulloch, J. A., *The Religion of the Ancient Celts*, Constable & Co., London, 1911.

Medicine Eagle, Brooke, *Buffalo Woman Comes Singing*, Ballantine Books, New York, 1991.

Monaghan, Patricia, *O Mother Sun!*, The Crossing Press, Freedom, California, 1994.

Monaghan, Patricia, *The New Book of Goddesses and Heroines*, Llewelyn Publications, St Paul, Minnesota, 1997.

Page, R.I., *Norse Myths*, University of Texas Press, Austin, Texas, 1990.

Palmer, Martin and Ramsay, Jay with Kwok, Man-ho, *Kuan Yin, Myths and Prophesies of the Chinese Goddess of Compassion*, Thorsons, an imprint of HarperCollins, London, 1995.

Palmer, Martin and Xiaomin, Zhao, *Essential Chinese Mythology*, Thorsons, an imprint of HarperCollins, London and New York, 1997.

Rees, Alwyn and Rees, Brinley, *Celtic Heritage, Ancient Tradition in Ireland and Wales*, Thames and Hudson, London, 1961.

Rolleston, T. W., *Myths and Legends of the Celtic Race*, Farrar & Rinehart Publishers, New York, (No date).

Squire, Charles, *Celtic Myth and Legend*, Newcastle Publishing Company, New York, 1975.

Wheeler, Post, *Sacred Scriptures of the Japanese*, Henry Schuman, Inc., New York, 1952.